SALVATION FOR ADDICTS

LEARNING TO UTILIZE THEWORD OF GOD TO BE PERMANENTLY SET FREE FROM ADDICTION

MARLON CHRISTMAS
A living Testimony

Table of Contents

Introduction

If you are currently reading this book, it is neither by chance nor circumstance, but rather a planned and calculated divine intervention. God has set forth and allowed a precise path that has leaded you to this precise and distinct moment.

The Lord knows everything about you! He knows your strengths and He knows your weaknesses. He is very much aware of your current struggles, yet regardless of your struggles, the Lord has had a profound plan for your life before you ever had a plan for yourself. Therefore, it was imperative that your plans fail in order for God's plans to prevail. He has never left your side, for God has purposefully protected you as you have endured every type of hardship seemingly known to mankind. I know the journey has been tough and you may have caused yourself and those around you a great deal of harm. I know from personal experience the pain and brokenness that is associated with addiction.

It makes you feel less than human as everything you once valued or cared about is replaced with guilt and shame. Life has become meaningless, you feel totally worthless, most of your family members have given up on you, and you have completely abandoned the idea of what friendship embodies. You are shipwrecked, you are alone and you know it is time to disembark; the storms of life are slowly engulfing you and you know it will not be much longer before you drown in the sea of your addictions. You have made many attempts to break free and swim ashore, but you are weighted down by your burdens and you cannot remain afloat. You have come to realize you cannot do it on your own, and you have given up. It feels like a really weak and hopeless moment, but it is the perfect and opportune time for God's power to be revealed in your life.

<u>**2Corinthians 2:9**</u> **"My grace is sufficient for you, for my power is made perfect in weakness."**

The power of God thrives in our weakest moments. He has allowed you to be crushed, torn in spirit, and completely broken. Everything the world has used to tear you down, God has divinely orchestrated to build you up and strength you for the task at hand. Brokenness is allowed by God as a tool to bring His wondering sheep back into His loving arms.

<u>**Matthew 11:28-30**</u> **"Come to me, all you who are weary and burdened, and I will give you rest. Take my yoke upon you and learn from me, for I am gentle and humble in heart, and you will find rest for your souls. For my yoke is easy and my burden is light."**

The brokenness you are experiencing is leading you up the staircase of humility and practical repentance. Humility is required in order for repentance to take place. Only through repentance can our relationship with God be restored, so prepare to embrace God as you never knew Him before and the prosperous life in which He has promised through His word.

God loves you and He wants you to know Him. His desire is to fill you with peace and give you a real life. God loves the people of this world so much that He gave His only son, Jesus so that everyone who has faith in Him will have eternal life. Jesus said, "I came so that everyone would have life, and have it in its fullest."

<u>**Acts 4:12**</u> **" Salvation is found in no one else, for there is no other name under heaven given to mankind by which we must be saved."**

Jesus has many names. "The Good Shepherd" is one of them. The Shepherd looks after the flock and protects them from danger. He knows you inside and out because He is the one who created you. Jesus wants to help you and enable you with a reliable source of strength (the Holy Spirit) that will aid and guide you in this life of recovery.

The saving grace of Jesus is at hand. He enables the blind to see, the death to hear, the mute to talk, the lame to walk, and He raises the dead to life. Therefore, without question, I am convinced He is able to deliver and set free those of us who are bound by the strongholds of addiction.

So what, you have problems; yes, you have struggles, but Christ recognizes our faults and is able to provide us with the necessary strength to overcome these apparent weaknesses.

Addiction was once your enemy, but from this point forward, it will be your strength and testimony of salvation to help and encourage others facing the same dilemma you once faced.

I am declaring in the name of Jesus Christ that you are set free and delivered from the strongholds of addiction! I am a living witness that all things are possible through Christ.

"True ambition is not what we thought it was. True ambition is the profound desire to live usefully and walk humbly under the grace of God."
<u>Bill W</u>

Know Your Enemy

It is very important that you study and understand what you are up against, for we cannot afford to remain ignorant. Addiction is simply a demonically inspired devise instituted by Satan in the vicious war waged against God. Satan has come against God in battle in hopes of capturing the souls of mankind. It is exceedingly important for us who were once addicts, but are now recovering addicts to develop a comprehensive knowledge about who the person of Satan is through the revelation of God's word and by the power of the Holy Spirit, which clearly exposes his character, and intentions.

- A third of the angels in heaven sided with Satan in their rebellion against God. They were cast down to the earth and given the authority to make war as Satan attempts to conquer mankind.
  (Revelation 12:7-12)
- Satan is constantly on the hunt seeking to devour God's children. **(1Peter5:8)**
- He is committed and whole heartedly devoted to the destruction of those who hold fast to their testimony about Jesus. **(Revelation 12:17)**
- He is skilled at disguising his true nature in hope of manipulating and deceiving the world.
  (2Corinthians 11:14)
- Satan is capable of taking people captive to do his will. **(2Timothy 2:26)**

- He is the spirit who is now at work in those who disobey God. **(Ephesians 2:2)**
- The Bible exposes him as a thief, with an agenda to steal, kill, and destroy all the children of God. **(John 10:10)**

The adversary has been exposed. The puppeteer of our addiction is no other than Satan himself; the bondage, the brokenness, and the uncontrolled nature of our lives is due to Satan. Spiritual warfare is real. The schemes of Satan are aimed to undermine our faith and destroy relational boundaries with God and render our lives unmanageable.

You are in a spiritual battle and that battle has led you into the stronghold of addiction, which is motivated by sin. The outcome of this battle will determine if the deception of Satan reigns in your life or the truth of Jesus.

The influence of Satan in our life is often disguised in pleasurable and exciting things that prove to be contrary to the word of God. He is capable of tempting us with sinful thoughts and ideas, but how we choose to respond to these sinful thoughts and ideas will determine if we are drawn into sin or not. Therefore, we must purpose in our hearts to leave all patterns of our addictive lifestyle behind by turning away from sin and addiction, and turning to God.

The rule of addiction in our lives has proven to have detrimental and demoralizing consequences. It was devastating for my family and friends to watch as I slowly tumbled down into a life filled with despair. They could not understand why I would continue to use drugs in spite of its devastating consequences. And neither could I.

Romans 7:15 **"I do not understand what do. For what I want to do I do not do, but what I hate I do."**

Jesus has already overcome the spiritual forces with which we battle today, for He acts to set things right in this life of contradiction. He knows we struggle daily with sinful influences. He also knows our hearts are troubled because we long to do right and not wrong. Addiction is simply an outward manifestation of an internal problem, a problem of the heart, but through our study of Biblical scriptures we are able to recognize what sin is, and how it disconnects us from God.

Ezekiel 36:26 **"I will give you a new heart and put a new spirit in you; I will remove from you your heart of stone and give you a tender and responsive heart."**

A change in our outward appearance in terms of behavior and conduct without renewing the mind or transforming our thought process is a promising road to relapse. The faulty heart must be replaced with a heart that is readily sensitive to the Holy Spirit.

The battle we fight is not with addiction; our battle is with sin. However, as we study God's word on how to deal with sin, we are better equipped to deal with the nature of our addiction. The most critical element for us as recovering addicts is to be aware that our battle requires that we operate in the Spirit. If we are to have any hope of being victorious over our struggles, it will be because of our reliance on the immeasurable power of God and the empowerment of the Holy Spirit.

2Corinthians 5:17 "**Therefore, if anyone is in Christ, he is new creation; the old has gone, the new has come.**"

Once you have let go and allowed God to lord over your life, you become a new creation. Your old self is gone. All your sins have been forgiven and you are free to start anew, but you must believe, believe it with all your heart. We have all sinned; we are all imperfect and have fallen short of God's glory, but you must not doubt that your heart has been changed by the power of the Holy Spirit. As recovering addicts, we can get back up, standing firm on God's word, and never again do we have to be subdued by addiction again.

Glory be to God that He lifts us up as we pray for His forgiveness, repenting of our sinful ways. As the sincere soul stumbles upon the stones set in his path by God's grace, he knows he can get up, brush himself off, repent, and right the error of his ways.

Proverbs 24:16 "**Though a righteous man falls seven times, he will get up, but the wicked will stumble into ruin.**"

So what, you may have relapsed once, maybe twice, or maybe you are like me and have fallen for the devices of Satan on numerous occasions. Nevertheless, a relapse is not the end of the world. We all have struggles and regret things in our past, but you are not your mistakes. It is not learning from your failures that is hindering your life. Your life is a lesson of experiences in which you are able to learn from past failures as well as God's word.

"The past is the past. Who or what we used to be doesn't matter anymore. What matters is who and what we are now and who and what we can become in the future."
Myles Munroe

God's grace is the blanket of our security. Therefore, no fall is ever permanent. God's faithfulness to His promise to keep those who believe allows us to be raised up each and every time. There is no reason to fret or worry even when you have fallen to adversity, simply put your trust in the Lord, for He will lift you up by His grace and mercy.

With every relapse, comes a tidal wave of deception from Satan. He has devices set in place for us to fall into and burden us down, to keep us lost, and in a state of confusion. Some of these devices are fear, guilt, shame, and resentment.

2Corintians 2:11 **"Lest Satan should take advantage of us; for we are not ignorant of his devices."**

In no way possible will you achieve victory on your own efforts. We can do nothing outside of Christ. Until you are ready to relinquish the pleasures of addiction, which is deliberately contrary to the character of Christ, you will not be able to experience true deliverance.

Satan's uses of devices are negative thoughts, certain television shows, corrupt music, circumstances, alcohol, drugs, and even certain reading material. All these devises are used to lead us astray and throw us off the path of righteousness. Satan never wants to see God's people in right standing with God. Therefore, he exposes us to things that are not consistent with God's word. This is why many of us fall due to our lack of knowledge of God's word.

Hosea 4:6 "My people are destroyed for lack of knowledge, because thou hast rejected knowledge..."

The best defense against these devices would be to familiarize yourself with the truth of God's word. As you begin to understand more about yourself, your struggles with addiction, and how Satan's use of certain devices to keep you burdened down, you need not be in a position to be caught off guard. Satan's advantage is based upon you being ignorant, but if you are aware of his methods to lead you astray, it becomes impossible to be deceived, and we are able to resist and not fall into temptation or any other scheme used to throw us off the path of being successful in this journey called life.

However, giving it to God does not necessarily mean everything is going to miraculously change overnight and all of your problems are suddenly going to disappear, but it does mean we can be more vigilant in the process of change as we begin to push away from sin and addiction, and on towards a life filled with grace and fulfillment.

God is in control of every situation. No matter how Satan attempts to harm us, God can use Satan's evil plans of destruction to work in our favor as long as we trust and obey Him. Start reading your Bible and then begin applying it to all areas of your life. The key to success is to read and apply the spiritual principles found in the Bible.

Set Free

If you are weary, sick, and tired of a life filled with despair, if you have tried every method of recovery, and you feel as though your life is absolutely hopeless, I want you to know that I have been there; I and numerous others have been to that breaking point. I hit bottom time and time again. I too have been deceived by every trick and scheme of addiction. Nevertheless, through God's grace and mercy, I found victory by knowing the life of Jesus Christ. I accepted Him into my life and I received the gift of the Holy Spirit, my strength, my comforter, and my friend.

Because of my acceptation of Christ, I am now set free from the oppression of my addiction. God's spirit now resides on the inside of me. Therefore, I am completely liberated as I take up my inward cross of self-denial as the changing grace of God teaches me to live soberly.

Luke 9:23 **"If any will come after me, let him deny himself, and take up his cross daily, and follow me."**

It is by God's grace that we are granted salvation, by learning to deny ourselves and live sober and righteous lives. So as we lift our eyes to heaven and give our hearts to Jesus, we are set free, free from bondage, free from oppression, free from despair, free from guilt, free from shame, free from every form of addiction, but more importantly, free from any deception that keeps us from the truth of knowing Jesus Christ.

The miracle is discovered within the promise of His word! The promise is that you shall know the truth and the truth will set you free. Jesus is that truth.

John 1:14 **"The word became flesh and made His dwelling among us, we have seen His glory the glory of the one and only son who came from the father full of grace and truth."**

Today, I walk in freedom, for where the spirit is there is peace, and joy. All the chains that once bound me are now broken. I truly do soar high on wings like an eagle.

Isaiah 40:31 **"But those who trust in the LORD will find new strength. They will soar high on wings like eagles. They will run and not grow weary. They will walk and not faint."**

God has made those of us who trust Him a promise because there are times when our own strength is not enough and in these trying times we are reminded to rely on God. There are sure to come times when we will grow weary, but the promise of God tells us that we will be lifted up and soar on wings like an eagle. Isn't it encouraging knowing that He will lift us up out of those weary places? We were never meant to endure the struggle alone. I highly recommend if you have not done so already that you invite God into the mist of your challenges because wherever God reside, His spirit resides also, and where the spirit reside, there is liberty.

2Corinthians 3:17 "Now the Lord is the Spirit, and where the Spirit of the Lord is, there is freedom."

Resisting Temptation

<u>**1 John 5:19**</u> **"We know that we are children of God, and that the whole world is under the control of the evil one."**

God is waiting to enable you, providing you the strength to resist temptation, and live a life of freedom. Our lives here on earth are like sheep living amongst wolves, but even though we are residing in the enemy's territory, we must choose to follow in the obedience of God's word. The Holy Spirit is our aid in exposing the deceptions and lies of Satan. He will help you to discern when Satan is trying to manipulate you.

 Having succumbed to the urges of temptation is a choice, just like any other choice in life. No matter how tempting the urge maybe, you have the power to resist. You can control them, for God has enabled you with the strength to resist any temptation the world has to offer by simply meditating on what God word says concerning your life, oppose to thoughts of yielding to the natural desires of the flesh.

<u>**Matthew 16:33**</u> **"I have told you these things, so that in me you may have peace. In this world you will have trouble. But take heart! I have overcome the world."**

God is very much aware of your current struggles when it comes to dealing with temptation. Nevertheless, He has given you a promise that you will not be tempted beyond what you are able to bare. I recommend that you pray for God to give you the strength to stand strong whenever temptation presents itself, and the wisdom to walk away from potentially unhealthy situations.

Hebrew 10:13 **"No temptation has overtaken you that is not common to man. God is faithful, and he will not let you be tempted beyond your ability, but with the temptation he will also provide the way of escape, that you may be able to endure it."**

One of the most successful ways of avoiding temptation is to change the people you hang around, the places you frequent and the self defeating thoughts that dominate your thinking, which in turn is stimulating your urge to do drugs. It is important not to make any provision for the flesh to fulfill its lust. You already know your own weaknesses. Therefore, if it is a certain place, do not go near it. If it is certain people in your life, than you need to change the people you are hanging out with. If having a pocket full of money is a trigger for you, then you may need to leave your money home or in a bank.

Peter 5:8 **"Be alert and of sober mind. Your enemy the devil prowls around like a roaring lion looking for someone to devour."**

I can remember many of times when I would put myself in compromise situations that where just plain unhealthy.

Whenever I would have any amount of clean time under my belt, I would feel so good about myself and my accomplishments that I would go wondering into those unhealthy environments just to show off. "Look I got myself together!" What I did not know is that getting clean is the easy part, but trying to remain clean is where the real battle began. Let's just say, I learned the hard way how important it was to change people, places and things. As I would walk into those unhealthy environments, my heart rate would instantly increase, and I would be well aware of what was happening. I knew I needed to get out as quick as possible, but a part of me wants to be there, and I'm not able to command myself to turn around and leave. And to my weakness, I would eventually succumb to the urge. It was not until the high was over, not until all my money had went up in smoke that the overwhelming sense of shame, guilt, and resentment would set in to tell me how worthless I was as a human being. I know now the only reason why I allowed myself to remain in such a compromising situation is because I did not have the power of the Holy Spirit as I do today. My fleshly desires controlled my every thought and action. No, I didn't want to get high, but I had no power to resist the urge, for I was a slave to my addiction.

Romans 7:18-20 "For I have the desire to do what is good, but I cannot carry it out. For I do not do the good I want to do, but the evil I do not want to do—this I keep on doing. Now if I do what I do not want to do, it is no longer I who do it, but it is sin living in me that does it."

Do we foolishly think that we can enjoy the facets of temptation without giving in to its urge? We are not strong enough to resist temptation alone. It is important to cry out to God for help and ask Him to show us the way out. Get Out Fast...

<u>**Hebrew 4:15**</u> **"For we do not have a high priest who is unable to empathize with our weaknesses, but one who have been tempted in every way, just as we are – yet he did not sin."**

Even Jesus had to face temptation, Jesus knew the persuasive power of temptation, but He also knew the perfect instructions of His Father. Jesus was able to conquer temptation by His knowledge of God's word. He Knew the Scriptures like He knew the back of His own hand. Jesus quotes from the word of God, using the scriptures as a sword for battle against temptation. His obedience to God is how He was able to overcome temptation and live victorious, and so can you.

> **Jesus' answer to temptation is "It is written in the scriptures..."**

God's word is a powerful weapon against temptation. Like any good warrior, we must train for battle. We already know what to expect and what to do before the battle comes, for the word of God teaches us. The word of God is our sword, and the more we familiarize ourselves with the scriptures, the more prepared we are for battle.

Satan comes to distort the truth of your life and to hinder the salvation and grace God has given you, but you must stand strong, resisting any urge that may be in opposition to God. As a child of God, we never give in because we know how to respond before temptation strikes.

James 1:12 "**Blessed is the man who remains steadfast under trial, for when he has stood the test he will receive the crown of life, which God has promised to those who love him.**"

At this stage in your recovery you may be facing numerous amounts of fear, but each fear has derived from the same source in which Satan has established a plot to deceive you with the intention of robbing you of God's promise. However, God will never forsake you. He is always right there to show us a way of escape.

Choices

Everything that has happened in your life is a reflection of a choice you have made. Therefore, if you want a different result, make a different choice. You may ask yourself: If God loves me so much, why does he allow me to make such stupid decisions. We call that the gift of free will. God will not force Himself upon anyone. He gives you the right to choose, and for every choice we make there are consequences. If I choose addiction, the consequence is death, but if I choose to accept God, the reward is eternal life.

Every morning I awake with a choice, and today I choose not to use, not to pick up or get high. And with each morning I awake, I depend on God to give me the necessary strength to commit to that choice. Just like me, you also have a choice to go on as best you can or turn your will over to the care of a power greater than yourself, greater than your situation or any so called addiction.

God granted you free will. He is giving you a choice. You can choose to willingly abide in His love and grace or you can continue living in a defeated lifestyle of addition. Though God has granted us the freedom of choice, He truly desires for us to choose Him.

Deuteronomy 30:19 "This day I call heaven and earth as witnesses against you that I have set before you life and death, blessings and curses. Now choose life, so that you may live and increase and the Lord your God will bless you …"

Not only does God give us a choice of blessings and curses, but he also provides the divine answer. "Choose Life!" Life is a choice and death is a decision. As you make the profound choice to choose life, it's not necessarily about what feels good, but rather about taking the necessary steps to build a better you. It is going to involve sacrifices, letting go things you once enjoyed, people you once hung out with, and places you can no longer frequent. It will become very important to play every decision all the way through in your head. When we deliberately succumb to temptation and sin, we are rejecting God's authority, and we instantly remove ourselves from His protection. Sin has extremely destructive consequences.

I have found drugs to be an extremely powerful enemy. It was not something that I could fend off on my own. I needed help! Addiction is a tool used by the Satan to keep God's chosen servants in bondage to sin, which brings about hopelessness. Satan wants you to feel like you have no hope. He is pleased when we commit to an unruly life of lies, deception, and idolatry. I discovered that help was indeed reaching out to me all along, and has been seeking my attention all my life. It was not until in the midst of my weakest moment, I would reach out to a Savior who had been patiently awaiting the day I would look to Him, and Him alone to relieve me of my anguish and affliction. Today, I realize that moment was my greatest strength.

<u>**2 Corinthians**</u> **12:9 "That is why, for Christ's sake, I delight in weaknesses, in insults, in hardships, in persecutions, in difficulties. For when I am weak, then I am strong."**

We cry out to God with the utmost sincerity when we are broken and hurting inside. We are able to surrender a part of ourselves that was impossible to let go when hanging on to a life of addiction. I had come to understand I was not only broken emotionally, but I was also broken spiritually. I had come to despise the man I had become. My life possessed a stench I could no longer bear, so I made one of the most relevant choices of my life in that moment of grief to completely surrender my will and life over to a loving, caring, and merciful God who is willing to forgive me, heal me and deliver me from the devastations of my addiction.

<u>**Psalms 119:71-72**</u> **"It was good for me to be afflicted so that I might learn your decrees. The law from your mouth is more precious to me than thousands of pieces of silver and gold."**

The choice of life over death is a choice that must be made daily in which I welcomely accept as I consider myself blessed to be able to wake up with such a choice. When I was using, I had no free will. My will was completely controlled by the use of drugs. It was absolutely impossible to resist its urge. I did not have the strength to say no, or the will to walk away.

Thanks to a caring God who refuses to give up on us, we have a way out of this bondage called addiction. Making the choice to accept Christ empowers us with the will to resist Satan and his devises and schemes of temptation.

The chains are broken, and tears of anguish are replaced with tears of joy, knowing we have a second chance at life.

"You are not fighting for victory—you are fighting from victory. This battle has already been won!"
<u>**Tony Evans**</u>

I embrace every morning as I awake with an overwhelming sense of joy, for I am able to recognize the miracle God has bestowed upon my life. It becomes so much easier to make the choice to remain clean and sober when you are able to recognize the miracles in your life. I have personally experienced hunger, homelessness, abandonment, and shame as a result of substance abuse. I know the brokenness that accompanies a life of addiction, and I know the hard work that comes along with overcoming that brokenness, but more notably, I know and understand the first step every addict must take in order to begin a life of recover, which is letting go and letting God.

Surrender

You may be experiencing the very same dilemma I was once faced with and you may be questioning, "Why is life so unfair? Why is everything such a struggle for me?" The "why" in such a question is used to inquire or seek an explanation for your circumstances. The truth of the matter is you were picked out to be picked on. It is important to understand who you are and why you are here. God created you for a specific purpose and the enemy (Satan) knows how important you are to the kingdom of God. When we are important to God, we become exceedingly important to Satan. God has created in you a good work and Satan has set out to destroy all the good works of God and that good work includes you.

Philippians 1:6 **"For I am confident of this very thing, that he who began a good work in you will perfect it until the day of Christ Jesus."**

The Lord has shaped you and crafted you for a unique place in His kingdom. No matter what your feelings may tell you, God has a place for you! Do your best to remain patient and prayerful. I want you to know that if you place yourself in the hands of God, that in His own time and in His own way, He will place you where you need to be. I know how frustrating it can become when it seems as if everyone has abandoned you, including God. You are left to fend for yourself, and you are not able to comprehend why your prayers are not being answered. When you have yielded to a mindset of this type of suffering, it is important to remember that you cannot trust your feeling.

Jeremiah 17:9 **"The heart is deceitful above all things, and desperately sick; who can understand it?"**

The devil will use your feeling to mislead you. When you were younger you may have been taught to trust your feeling. However, drugs are a mind altering substance. Therefore, your mind, thoughts and feelings are not currently healthy. Even though you are surrounded by light, you just can't seem to see it. We need to realize that our state of affairs are not an indication as to rather God is with us or not. The Bible assures us that God will never leave us or forsake us. When you have decided to let go and you allow the difficult times to pass, you will then look back upon your life with a joy, knowing that God was holding you safely in his hands the whole entire time.

Luke 6:47-48 **"I will show you what he is like who comes to me and hears my words and puts them into practice. He is like a man building a house, who dug down deep and laid the foundation on rock. When a flood came, the torrent struck that house but could not shake it, because it was well built."**

When you are threatened by the storms of addiction, when impeding urges threatens to obstruct your everyday living, your survival will depended on how strong your foundation is. Your victory will depends on how well you put into practice the scriptures studied from the Bible.

It was not until many years later that I would grow to understand why I was faced with some of the most devastating circumstances life could throw at me. I had to come to the realization that every day when I would awake each morning, I was blessed with a choice, a choice to continue in the misery of addiction or the choice to turn my will over to the care of a power greater than myself.

It had become socially acceptable amongst my peers and associates to be involved in the use of drugs and alcohol at that time. When I first started, it all seemed like a lot of fun, just a simple recreational enjoyment. I never had a clue about where the out-come of such behaviors would lead me. What once was just an every now and then enjoyment now became a need just to feel normal. My addiction was growing and my demons were becoming increasingly more powerful every day. Life slowly started becoming unmanageable. I had begun to isolate myself from my family and those who truly cared about me. In all honesty, I had become ashamed of the person I now saw in the mirror. My whole appearance had changed. I was completely lost in my addiction. Drug had taken my entire life away from me in practically no time at all. Every time I would attempt to bounce back, or get clean and sober, my addiction would show up just to knock me back down and tell me, I am nobody. I really needed someone I could turn to, someone who could help. I had lost all I had and any sense of who I was. My spirit was broken. I felt abandoned and lonely. Life had backed me into a corner and addiction was squeezing out every ounce of life I had left.

There, at that moment, I knew I had no control over my life. I knew I would die. I was ready to give myself over to death. Time and time again, I had attempted to pull myself up, but with no avail, and I was just ready to give up, not caring rather I live or die. It was at that precise moment, I cried out to God, "Why me?"

Instead of answering my question, I was presented with a new dilemma of 'what" what are you going to do about it? Would I carry on as best I could or would I accept the loving grace of a merciful God willing to restore me and mend together all the broken pieces of my life?

"I thank the Lord that even though things were so wrong in my life, I was finally brought to the realization of what all those struggles were about. There are some wonderful things from your painful past, things with a beauty you may not have realized at the time."
<u>Ravi Zacharias</u>

Destiny had taken its course and all and my circumstances were allowed that I might get to this very point in my life of total and complete surrender. I was tired, broken, and abandoned. I was left with no one else to turn to. Therefore, I cried out to the only ear that would hear, "God!"

Don't ever get the impression that God is some kind of escape goat or crutch that people use as means of giving up. It is not!! It is neither defeat nor resignation. Giving a situation over to God is not quitting, but only a simple means of surrendering. You have come to a place of deep acceptance that you are unable to deal with the situation on your own and that you are totally powerless. Your only option is to surrender your circumstances over to a power greater than yourself. The first step to humility is to surrender. Surrender is an expression of maturation. As we surrender our self-will over to God, we let go of confounding distortions of who the world says we are and we embrace the truth about who God says were are.

1 John 4:4 "But you belong to God, my dear children. You have already won a victory over those people, because the spirit who lives in you is greater than the spirit who lives in the world."

God had been my greatest strength all along and I never knew it. This was a battle I never had to fight alone, for the battle had already been won when Jesus had given himself up on the cross for the sins of the entire world. I only needed to make the choice to accept Him as my personal savior. I had to learn that my fight was not against those around me, or the drugs itself; it was much bigger than that. I was caught in the middle of spiritual warfare.

Ephesians 6:12 "**For we are not fighting against flesh-and-blood enemies, but against evil rulers and authorities of the unseen world, against mighty powers in this dark world, and against evil spirits in the heavenly places.**"

This scripture reminds us that the true nature of our battle is spiritual; it is a spiritual warfare. Satan is at war with God's people. It is a war because these evil forces use vigorous and hostile strategies to stop God's will in our lives. Satan wants to see us filled with despair, hopelessness, anger, and guilt. He lies to us, engaging us in the appealing use of drugs and alcohol so that we miss the opportunities that God has for us as he shrewdly seeks to destroy our life. Currently, your self-control is under attack and Satan lures us with tempting pleasures of the world that are hard to refuse. His desire is to lead us away from the knowledge of Christ. When we fall into temptation, we are drawn away from God and that is when we become powerless. We must pray to God who gives us the strength to over-come and not live in fear of failure.

Matthew 26:41 "**Watch and pray so that you will not fall into temptation. The spirit is willing, but the flesh is weak.**"

Satan loves to implement fear because he knows it is a weakness. He is committed to a perilously strategic plan of destroying our relationship with God and His son Jesus. He wants to destroy our marriages and isolate us from family, friends and the Church, for by doing so, he knows we are more easily influenced, more easily oppressed, and more easily controlled. He knows that if he can destroy your mind, he will destroy your spirit, and if he is able to destroy your spirit, he will have accomplished his main agenda, which is to totally separate us from the love of God.

I would always fall for the alluring temptation that using drugs was fun or that its pleasures were so overwhelmingly good that I needed it, so that I could forget about all my problems. Subconsciously, I was being manipulated and mislead by evil principalities. How much fun is that to go from one meaningless high to the next while knowingly ruining my life? Spiritual warfare is real. Disguising itself in the form of drugs, and alcohol was Satan's way of leading me to a life filled with hopelessness and eventually death. I had to learn that I alone had no power to wrestle with the schemes of Satan, but more importantly, without surrendering unto Christ, I would never be any match for him. By accepting Christ, I found the necessary strength to resist, the strength to stand firm, and the (knowledge) to know Satan has no power over me.

Now, I want you to think back about all the adversities that you have been through, and I would like to help you understand just "why" you were allowed such harsh and confounding circumstances. All that Satan intended for bad, I want you to see that God has brought about a good outcome. All your hardship and circumstances were purposefully allowed to build in you the changes necessary for your purpose in God's kingdom. For instance, without abandonment, you would not have built up a sense of independence and co-dependence on God in which you are currently discovering is essential for those of us hoping to live victoriously over addiction. Each and every obstacle in our lives was allowed for the purpose of building a uniquely specific character trait needed to fulfill our ultimate purpose in the journey of life. God allowed you to be broken so that He might build you up. He allowed your heartbreaks so that your eyes would be open to the one and only true and faithful love that can only be found in the love of Christ. He allowed your shame to establish humility and break through your pride in order to develop in you a repentant heart. Every seemingly harsh experience is now a blissful blessing and testimony that can be used to help and encourage someone else who may be experiencing similar circumstances.

Therefore, when bad things happen and you feel confused or confound with its understanding, it is important to trust the process. We need to see it as a time for learning and trusting God by changing certain behaviors and activities that are wrong, such as the use of drugs, alcohol, and other life dominating activities that interfere with the promises God has placed in our hearts, and when it is all said and done, we can look back and see that our trials were necessary. We are better, new and improved. We are wiser, gifted with the spirit of discernment. We are stronger, not easily shaken, and ultimately God is glorified!

Romans 8:28 "And we know that in all things God works for the good of those who love him, who have been called according to his purpose."

In the Bible, the book of Job teaches us many things about Satan. Job's friends did not blame Satan for job's troubles, but insinuated that God was the cause of Job's suffering, but they were wrong. God simply allowed Job's circumstances. Therefore, it is important to keep in mind God is never the cause of our suffering. However, God will allow our circumstance in hopes of testing, refining and building a bank of foundational spiritual character to be used in building and establishing the kingdom of God. Will you surrender?

Isaiah 48:10 "I have refined you, though not as silver; I have tested you in the furnace of affliction."

Life is a journey, and the ups and downs we experience are simply lessons meant to promote growth and build character, character that will manifest into spiritual fruit. This is not an easy process because it requires that you surrender your self-will and put all your focus on Christ. Our thoughts must be moved from our own will to God's will. When you realize that there is supernatural strength available to you from above, then your perspective on life will change. Only then does the proper perspective become unmistakenly clear as you become better equipped to make sense out of everyday living, knowing that God will give you the strength to persevere, for it is only by the strength of God we are capable of finally overcoming the addiction that once plagued our lives.

Turning your will and your life over to the care of God gives you a tremendous advantage. Life becomes easier because you no longer lean on your own understanding, but are now trusting in the divine wisdom of God, allowing Him to lead and guide your steps through adverse times. He is willing to provide all your needs, for in God, we find rest, we find peace, but more importantly, we find salvation.

If you are not willing to surrender and allow God to take the helm of your shipwrecked life, then how else are you going to love, obey, and completely trust that God has your best interest at heart? Without surrendering to God, how else are you going to weather the storms and the trials that wreak havoc in your life? If you are to overcome discouragement, disappointments and the disillusions that plague your thoughts, you must commit to the most important step of all, total and complete surrender.

"No matter what evil you have experienced in the past, that experience should not hold you hostage for the rest of your life."
Pastor John Gray

Running to God is not a sign of weakness; it is a sign of significant strength as you peel off defect after defect in which you have come to identify in your present character.

It is time to put aside selfishness, stop looking for others to blame and stop justifying your destructive behaviors. It is time you take personal responsibility for ever thought, decision, and action you take.

I know all too well because I been there. I too had a problem with accepting responsibility. I would blame everyone else for all the problems going on in my life. Every time I would relapse, I would find someone else to place the blame on other then myself. Every argument was an excuse to get high. Every life disappointment was a reason to pick up. That's the sickness of addiction. When the urge to do drugs or have a drink becomes overwhelming, it will certainly assist you in your efforts to find liable excuses to get high. Nevertheless, blame is a learned behavior that can be unlearn by accepting responsibility for your own actions. Therefore, instead of spending time and energy on blame, move into a new thought process of accepting responsibility for yourself and visualize what a new life without drugs and alcohol can actually look like. Begin by praying "Not my will God, but Yours," by doing so, you are making preparations to align yourself with a power greater than yourself. By surrendering, you are allowing God to manifest the miracle He already predestined for your life to take fruit. I find it comforting knowing that God is willing to take the travesties of our situations and turn them into something good and purposeful.

When I decided to completely surrender my will over to the care of God, I did it from the very innermost depth of my heart and soul, and this must also be your ultimate goal, letting go and letting God; then, I had to attain a comprehensive understanding of scriptures by study and meditation. As I began talking to God, God's word began to speak to my heart and mind. He gave me the guidance I needed to overcome addiction and the key to successfully attain salvation.

<u>Psalm 119:9-11</u> "How can a young person stay pure? By obeying your word and following its rules. I have tried my best to find you don't let me wander from your commands. I have hidden your word in my heart that I might not sin against you."

It is imperative that once you completely let go and surrender to God, you by no means relinquish that surrender. Once you begin to yield any small amount of that total surrender, you slowly begin opening the door for addiction to creep back into your life. I speak from past experience when I say, "you will begin to endure the very same struggles you were delivered from as your state of mind reverts back to a sick and demented sense of selfishness all over again." The devil loves to see your mind in chaos because he knows you will lose sight of hope. It is important to mediate on God's word because it will remind you that God has a plan for your life.

I know firsthand what if feels like to live as a defeated recovering addict. I went through all the motions. I prayed, attended service, and I also attended a few NA meeting, but what I had yet to do was study the Bible vigorously in search of answers to my addiction problem. I had yet to meet and accept the God who stood behind those words reaching out to me with sincere love and unquestionable compassion.

Isaiah 65:2 **"I have stretched out My hands all day long to a rebellious people, Who walk in a way that is not good, According to their own thoughts."**

I did not understand the love involved in the sacrifice of His beloved son Jesus for my sake. I was just a lukewarm church attendee with minimal devotion. I didn't live for his will and purpose. I was naive to the dangers that surrounded my everyday living. It is not enough to accept Christ and not seek to understand who He is or who I had become in Him.

John 17:3 **"And this is eternal life, that they know you, the only true God, and Jesus Christ whom you have sent."**

The knowledge of God leads us out of the domain of darkness, for if anyone be in Christ, he has become a new creation. Once we have an encounter with God, it literally transforms us for the rest of our lives. You talk differently, you behave differently and you will respond to your circumstances differently because by faith you have come to believe in the power of God and the person of the Holy Spirit. Power over addiction is knowing who you are in Christ. The knowledge of Jesus is the key to being set free from addiction, hate, resentment, guilt, self pity, egotism, insecurities, dishonesty, negative thinking, fear, and anxiety.

Today, I clearly understand. I understand that every recovering addict faces two deadly enemies on a day to day basis. The first enemy is our carnal nature, and the second enemy is Satan himself. It was through the carnality of my flesh in which I would give in to those impulsive urges and desires as I continually hungered for more and more drugs.

Corinthians 15:31 "**The canal nature is extremely selfish and demand attention; therefore, the canal nature must be put to death daily.**"

The only way to overcome the carnal nature, which is also known as fleshly desires, is by completely surrendering our will over to God. By doing so, we are able to put to death the deeds of our sinful nature, which means you can never be too busy to kneel before God in prayer. You must always make time to study God's word and meditate on the scriptures. You must allow this routine to slowly become a way of life in hopes of sustain a sense of peace that surpasses all understanding. If properly implemented, you will notice an inner strength that gives you power over the addiction that once kept you in bondage. Rather than listening to yourself or suggestive thoughts ordered by Satan in moments of temptation, you will speak to yourself with Biblical truths as you utilize the strength of the Holy Spirit to sustain you; then you will never have to succumb to addictive urges ever again. But you must surrender!

Romans 8:12-13 "Therefore, dear brothers and sisters, you have no obligation to do what your sinful nature urges you to do, for if you live by its dictates you will die, but if by the power of the Holy Spirit you have put to death the deeds of the sinful nature, you will live…"

God is patiently waiting to embrace the yielded and surrendered heart of our soul. I admit I was not always thankful. As a sinner, I was blind to the presence of God in my life, but now as I look back and think about how God maneuvered some of the most difficult situations in my life, I am truly thankful. Many of God's actions were chastisement set in place to redirect me from committing sin.

Hebrew 12:6 "Because the Lord disciplines those he loves and he punishes everyone he accepts as a son."

If you honestly take a good look at your life, you will see that God has walked every step of this journey with you in hopes of guiding you back on the path to righteousness. It is certainly not luck that you are currently reading this book. It is not luck or by chance that you are now seeking the truth. It is God! His signature is all over your life.

It's time to let go, surrender, and allow God's purpose for your life to be revealed. The time is now, so if there are any difficulties that have been troubling you-let it go. Any addiction that has kept you in bondage-let it go. Any heartache that is troubling you on the inside-let it go. Give it all to God and allow the transformation of your new Christ filled life to begin.

Insanity

Insanity is repeating the same mistakes over and over again and expecting a different result. Ideally, if you are hoping to change your situation, you are going to have to get in the habit of making better decisions. I am over 40 years of age and I am a recovering addict. I am recovering my dignity, my virtues, my honor, my self-respect, and my sense of purpose. I started using in my late teens. My life has been a living rollercoaster ever since. I have been up and I have been down. I can say from repeated occurrences that I have been face to face with insanity. It is not enjoyable, nor is it rewarding, for it drains the life out of you. It leaves you desperate, bewildered, discouraged, and dejected.

Insanity would have me to believe that if I carefully and strategically planed my next relapse, that no harm would come of it. However, the results proved to always be the same, handcuffs. I would just sit there, all burnt out, feeling like a dimwit, wondering what went wrong from the inside of a jail cell. Once again, I would be left to drown in my misery. Yet, every time I made the decision to pick up, I would somehow come to believe and expect a different result. It is like running your head into a brick wall, repeatedly. You know it is going to hurt, you know it's going to leave a scar, yet regardless of the damage, you just continue ramming your head against that same wall as if to expect something different aside from pain and anguish.

Not only have I tried it, I have lived it. I have hit that wall time and time again. I can tell you from experience and a profound since of maturity that the results are always the same, shame and guilt. With every use, these same resentments would come rushing back at me to attack what life and dignity I had left. The results are inevitable if you continue as you have; unavoidably, you will face three detrimental outcomes, Jails, Institution, and Death!

I have been arrested on several occasions due to my addiction to drugs. I have been to prison twice and the sad part about it all is that I always knew exactly where I would end up when making the decision to get high. See, I was never a person that could go out and simply get loaded for a couple of hours or put boundaries or limits on the amount I would spend or use in a single night. Unfortunately for me, a night of getting high could last weeks or even years. I had to have it all. I was all gas and no breaks. With my addictive personality, I would always have to have more and more. I would stay out until I would practically drop dead or end up in jail once again. There were times when I would pray for jail because I needed it to stop. I had no control to make it stop on my own. My body wanted more, and I just could not will myself to let go, stop and get the help I needed. I was headed for death! But going to jail would rescue me for a short period of time, allowing me to get off that never-ending rollercoaster of addiction. I would actually be grateful for my arrest. I usually saw it as an opportunity to slow down and start my life over again.

However, the insane part is that whenever I would pull myself together or get my life back on track that overwhelming sense of anxiety would hit me all over again. I would have an unrelenting urge to get high and I just could not shake it. I used to think that the coping skills I was taught was not working, but later came to understand it was me not putting what coping skills I had learned into practice. In my weakness, Satan would bombard me with all sorts of negative thoughts. I would begin telling myself all over again that just going out and partying for one night is not going to cause any harm.

Have you ever heard the term "One is too many and a thousand is never enough." Well, in my case, one was surely too many and no matter how much I used, it was never enough to satisfy my cravings. I had to have it at all cost, and so I talked myself into using once again, and once again, I came face to face with insanity, doing the same thing and expecting a different result.

In life, unlike chess, the game continues after checkmate and losing the battle, does not necessarily mean you have lost the war. Though Satan is out to distort the truth about who you are in Christ, a heart surrendered unto God does not sit back and except his lies.

It is imperative you be able to discern godly thoughts from the thoughts Satan will try to plant in your thinking. When those subtle thoughts of using or getting high comes roaring back, it is the enemy planting seeds in your mind. Temptation is only a test! A test of your loyalty, a test of your strength, and a test of your faith, and with the passing of every test, comes an unexpected blessing from a kind and merciful God.

I never said this journey would be easy. It takes a surrendered mind and heart, and a commitment to study God's word. The word of God is power! It is power over Satan, power over negative thoughts and power over addiction. That power comes by declaring what God has promised you in His word. Many of times when we find ourselves in turmoil, we tend to lose hope, but when we remind ourselves that God has a plan for our lives and wants us to prosper, we are then reassured, knowing we can rest in a sense of peace and live victoriously.

James 1:8 **"A double minded man is unstable in all his ways."**

I consider it to be double minded when you want to live a clean and sober lifestyle, yet you refuse to relinquish the lifestyle that keeps you in bondage. Either you are going to be drawn in by your urges to get high or you are going to be drawn in by your desire to remain clean and sober, but you cannot have them both. Double mindedness and insanity go hand and hand. How many times have you cried out to God to get you out of a particular situation and promised to never do it again? However, as soon as you were delivered, you ran right back out and did the same thing without regard for the promise you made to God. It truly is insane the amount of hurt and pain we put ourselves through, thinking it is going to be any different the next time around. Breaking News: It will always be the same good feeling in the beginning, with the same devastating results in the end. The instant gratification that comes with using never outweighs the destructive lifestyle that comes with it.

Insanity is a form of irrational thinking and behavior that can be changed. The time is now to make the decision to abandon every behavior that keeps you in bondage to addiction. You do not have another relapse left in you. The consequences are too great. Besides, why suffer such an epic plunge when you have been exposed to the knowledge that can help you to overcome addiction and save your life.

If you have not already, now is the perfect time to come to God, accepting Jesus with an open heart and sound mind. He is listening! Take the time to confess your sins, your weakness and submit all that you are to Him. You have traveled a long and strenuous journey, once filled with despair, dejection and desolation due to not only the use of drugs, but also due to ignorance of the truth. That burdensome journey is now over. I would like you to look forward with expectancy to a new journey in which you have been forgiven, a journey where you now have hope that it does and it will get better. God is about to do extraordinary things in your life. Are you ready? Are you willing? It is your decision and only you can make it.

Remember, God has been reaching out to you since the day you were born that you would receive His Son Jesus as your personal Lord and Savior. Now you can begin the life He has planned for you. Step by step God will lead you to what He has chosen for you. He will show you the way and will teach you each day as you grow spiritually and become the person He planned for you to be.

I know that God can bring you through any challenge you face. You can receive Christ right now.

Revelation 3:20 "Behold, I stand at the door and knock. If anyone hears My voice and opens the door, I will come in to him and dine with him, and he with Me."

Would you like to respond to His invitation? Here's how

Romans 10:9 "If you declare with your mouth, "Jesus is Lord," and believe in your heart that God raised him from the dead, you will be saved."

The Holy Spirit will also come to live on the inside of you as a result of accepting Jesus as your personal Lord and Savior.

Acts 2:38 "Repent and be baptized, every one of you, in the name of Jesus Christ for the forgiveness of your sins. And you will receive the gift of the Holy Spirit."

It is through the power of the Holy Spirit we are able to develop Christ like character, which is the key to lasting transformation. Our part is to meditate upon God's Word, so we can learn about His character and apply His principles. Then, instead of gratifying our sinful urges, we are now able to make wise and rational decisions.

Transformed

As a recovering addict, you have made the decision to turn your will over to the care of God. Therefore, spiritually you have become a new person, recreated and transformed to conform to the likeness of Christ by the power of the Holy Spirit.

Isaiah 43:17 "Do not remember the former things, nor consider the things of old."

At this stage of your recover, you will have made up your mind to never go back to your old ways, old friends, or old hang outs. Recovery is allowing yourself to be transformed. However, transformation is something you have to want and that intense want has to exceed your minds tendency to rationalize.

Romans 12:2 "Don't copy the behavior and customs of this world, but let God transform you into a new person by changing the way you think. Then you will learn to know God's will for you, which is good and pleasing and perfect."

Each and every day we come across thoughts that need to be put in check. These are the thoughts that do not line up with God's truth.

For example, hate, anger, jealousy, unforgiveness, lust, envy, and selfishness; these are unhealthy thoughts that you should not be having. Satan will use thoughts like these to coerce you back into a life of addiction. Your sinful nature reaches out to the things of this world that are not pleasing to God. Therefore, by renewing your mind and lining up your thoughts with the scriptures, your sinful desires will change into a strong conviction to please God.

2Corinthians 10:5 **"We demolish arguments and every pretension that sets itself up against the knowledge of God, and we take captive every thought to make it obedient to Christ."**

One of the many names of Satan is The Tempter, for he is masterful at tempting us with sinful thoughts in hopes of drawing us into sin. However, Jesus was just as masterful at utilizing scriptures to fight back against tempting thoughts. We are called to be an imitator of Christ.

1 Peter 2:21 **"For to this you have been called, because Christ also suffered for you, leaving you an example, so that you might follow in his steps."**

Therefore, if you find yourself reflecting on a thought that you realize is contrary to the mind of Christ, such as the urge to drink, use drugs, manipulate, lie or deceive, I suggest that you rebuke the spirit that is causing the tempting thought, taking the thought captive and make it obedience to Christ because if you choose to entertain such a thought, you will eventually develop an emotion about it, which will eventually compel you to take action and a devastating relapse is soon to follow.

Satan is exceedingly happy when we convert back to our old ways, conforming once again to active addiction. He uses our own sinful desires against us, and for that very reason, we take those unhealthy thoughts and we line them up with the word of God, refocusing our minds on everything that is true, noble, right, pure, lovely, admirable, excellent, and worthy of praise. These are the type of thoughts you want meditating in your mind when temptation arises or when life's challenges come at you.

James 4:7-8 **"Submit yourselves then to God. Resist the devil, and he will flee from you. Come near to God and he will come near to you."**

As recovering addicts, many of us easily give up on the good fight. We give in and conform to a way of life that is unbecoming of the morals we were brought up to believe. As you very well know, addiction is a very powerful and cunning enemy. How many times have you sought happiness and enjoyment through the use of drugs, only to find anguish and miser? The problem is lack of mental discipline, allowing ourselves to be controlled by the negative impulse planted by Satan, but until we change our way of thinking, we will continually chase after these things that cause disruption and confusion in our lives. It is time to reverse this cycle. Instead of relying on drugs and alcohol to elate us, we must begin relying on God and all the riches and favor that comes along with our newly discovered transformation. We no longer look at life based on the negative, but rather the positive. It is time to transform your cycle of thinking. There is nothing too impossible for you to accomplish now that you have surrendered your will and life over to the care of God. You are more than conquers now that you have surrendered, and you are now able to stand tall and live victoriously over your addiction.

Temptation is no longer a factor in your life as those seeds of doubt planted by the enemy are no longer an issue. From this point forward, you will not turn to drugs or alcohol when you are seeking escape from life's dilemma. You will now turn to the source of your strength, God!

Transformation takes place when we involve ourselves in the study of the scriptures. You will learn that the Bible is full of examples of men and women who utilized their faith in God to overcome the trials in their life. For every problem we face, the Bible has an example of how God was able to deliver the suffering and the afflicted, so if you are willing to trust that the promises of God are real and that God is who he says he is, then you too will find deliverance from addiction.

Being that God's love is unconditional, He loves you just the way you are, but He loves you way too much to let you stay that way. It is time to banish the limitations you have placed on what God is capable of doing in your life because

God has a plan for your life that is bigger and better than anything you could ever imagine.

<u>Peter 5:8-9</u> **"Be self-controlled and alert. Your enemy the devil prowls around like a roaring lion looking for someone to devour. Resist him, standing firm in the faith, because you know that your brothers throughout the world are undergoing the same kind of sufferings."**

Self-control is the ability to control impulses and reactions. As a recovering addict, you are called to be self-disciplined. Having self-control allows you to overcome addictive, obsessive, and compulsive behaviors. It also helps you to reject negative feelings and thoughts that might prove to be self-destructive; in turn, allowing your life to be transformed.

<u>Ephesians 4:22-24</u> **"To put off your old self, which belongs to your former manner of life and is corrupt through deceitful desires, and be renewed in the spirit of your minds, and put on the new self, created after the likeness of God in the true righteousness and holiness."**

When we transform our way of thinking and our personal views of ourselves, it will eliminate feelings of hopelessness, and brings about a sense of balance to our lives. It strengthens our self-esteem and self-confidence as we begin to take responsibility for our actions and become productive members of society.

Luke 4:13 "When the devil had finished tempting Jesus, he left him until the next opportunity came."

Keep in mind that Satan is waiting. He is monitoring our activities and setting up circumstances in which to tempt us. His goal is to destroy anything godly that lives inside of you. He cannot wait to put your new found faith to the test. He will set stumbling blocks before you, and many distractions to push you off course. There will be urges and temptation, but you have power over your fleshly desires and thoughts. True enough, you can't control what happens around you, but you can control how you choose to react. It is important to be mindful of your perspective, for the proper perspective allows you to conquer the world around you and what and how you think will ultimately determine what choices you make in life.

Therefore, watch your thoughts, for they become words. Watch your words, for they become actions. Watch your actions, for they become habits. Watch your habits, for they become your character. Seeing life with the proper perspective can only happen through the knowledge of God's word in which you learn that even though you are not able to control your circumstances, you are able to respond to your circumstances in a healthy Christ like manor.

Our mind generates all types of thoughts and to be honest, not all of them are going to be good, but when you come to the revelation that you no longer have to act on nor entertain these thoughts, you eliminate a lot of unnecessary stress out of your life. The way we think impacts the way we feel and the way we feel impacts our behaviors. Negative thoughts tend to get in the way of us moving forward. We have all had bad experiences and disappointments in life, but you cannot let that get in the way of your recovery. Thoughts such as hopelessness, shame, fear, guilt can keep us from committing to the necessary steps that will improve our lives and keep us in a continued cycle of poor decision making, but when you decide to focus on the positive, it is going to help you begin to work through a lot of difficult situations. When I actively choose to remain dedicated, loyal, and committed to God's word, I was able to steer clear of negative thinking and align my heart with God's perfect will for my life. When we allow God's word to penetrate our heart and mind, we are then transformed. The chains of bondage are broken as we place our faith, hope, and trust in Jesus.

Faith Hope Trust

"Without faith, hope and trust, there is no promise for the future, and without a promising future, life has no direction, no meaning and no justification."
Adlin Sinclair

Faith is a very powerful tool and only comes by the hearing of God's word. Jesus Himself said that even with just a little amount of faith, we can move mountains. Faith is like a muscle, the more you exercise it, the more it grows, for it is the power that enables us to do great and mighty things by the power of the Holy Spirit.

Without faith, we would not believe in God. We would not trust that He listens to our prayers and responds in our best interest.

Hebrew 12:1 "Now faith is the substance of things hoped for, the evidence of things not seen."

To have hope is to live with the expectancy that God will eventually turn everything around and bring you up out of the storm that has you shipped wrecked.

A life without hope *is* a scary concept. I know, I nearly died without it. But today, I am fully alive, for hope has changed my life and my hope is Jesus.

Lamentations 3:25 "The LORD is good to those whose hope is in him, to the one who seeks him."

When times are tough and things are not going our way is when we find it the most difficult to trust God. Trust is not an easy thing to come by, but it is one of the most essential parts of our relationship with God. We develop a God trusting heart by meditating on Scripture as we rely less on ourselves and more on Christ. Trusting in the Lord is the only path to recovery. He willingly pours his Spirit into the hearts of those who trust Him.

Jeremiah 17:7-8 "But blessed is the man who trusts in the LORD whose confidence is in him. He will be like a tree planted by the water that sends out its roots by the stream. It does not fear when heat comes; its leaves are always green. It has no worries in a year of drought and never fails to bear fruit."

By now you have endured a lifetime of experiences, and you probably feel discouraged and dejected by all that you have gone through, but today, I assure you that these problems are only temporary as God awaits with open arms to embrace you.

Jeremiah 29:11-12 "For I know the plans I have for you," declares the LORD, "plans to prosper you and not to harm you, plans to give you hope and a future. Then you will call upon me and come and pray to me, and I will listen to you."

I have personally found the Bible to be my strength in helping me to resolve many of my life challenges. Therefore, the next time you are feeling dejected or discouraged, turn to the scriptures and be edified knowing that God's unfailing love is with you always.

Romans 5:5 "**And hope does not disappoint us, because God has poured out his love into our hearts by the Holy Spirit, whom he has given us.**"

Reading and memorizing scriptures is one thing, but do you truly believe them with all your heart? It is important not to let discouragement or doubt have rule over you. You have been called according to His purpose and will for your life, and the best place for anyone who is struggling with addiction is at the center of God's will. God is the only person whom you will ever know who will not disappoint you, who will never fail you, and who will whole heartedly love you unconditionally.

Romans 15:13 "**May the God of hope fill you with all joy and peace as you trust in him, so that you may overflow with hope by the power of the Holy Spirit.**"

I often wonder why we allow ourselves to endure so much pain and frustration before we finally give up and turn to God for help. Then, I began to realize that sometimes it takes a broken spirit to truly appreciate God. No matter how bad your troubles or circumstance, no matter how broken you feel, God is able to pick up the pieces of your life and make you whole again. He has the ability to turn your situation around. As you submit and open your heart to His unfailing love, God gives you the power of the Holy Spirit, which in turn helps you to recover from a once shattered life. The Holy Spirit is going to be a big factor in helping you make the proper choices as you continue forward with your life.

John 16:13 **"When He, the Spirit of truth, comes, He will guide you into all the truth; for He will not speak on His own initiative, but whatever He hears, He will speak; and He will disclose to you what is to come."**

The Holy Spirit has been given to those of us with faith, hope and trust in Jesus. God already knew that we could not make it on our own. Therefore, instead of trying to overcome on our own, Gods ask us to rely solely on Him as He builds self-control, patience, peace, kindness, joy, and love within our hearts to be reflected in our everyday living. The Holy Spirit is used to produce the character of God in every believer. Before Jesus died, He promised He would ask God to send us another counselor by the name of the Holy Spirit.

John 14:16 **"And I will ask the Father, and he will give you another advocate to help you and be with you forever..."**

The Holy Spirit is what draws us near to God, encourages us to pray and spread the good news about who Jesus is.

The Holy Spirit will help you to become conscience of sin as you are made consciously aware of immoral and deceitful thoughts, forever reminding you of right and wrong, and brings forth the fruit of the spirit in your life.

<u>**Galatians 5:22-23**</u> **"But the fruit of the Spirit is love, joy, peace, forbearance, kindness, goodness, faithfulness, gentleness and self-control. Against such things there is no law."**

Because of your decision to accept Jesus Christ, God will begin cultivating seeds of spiritual fruit already planted in your spirit. Within you shall live a sense of peace that surpasses all understanding and no matter how difficult your circumstances, you will allow nothing to disrupt the joy and peace that now resides inside your heart. You can call upon the spirit to help you in all things. To overcome addiction on your own may be impossible, but life through the spirit gives you a supernatural ability to stand strong, resist temptation, and overcome addiction. The more you press into the heart of God, praying and reflecting on God's word, the more you will begin to reflect the character of God, behaving in accordance with God's will for your life.

<u>**Acts 1:8**</u> **"But you shall receive power when the Holy Spirit has come upon you; and shall be my witnesses..."**

The Holy Spirit is with you always. Where ever you go, He is with you because He lives on the inside of you to help you and comfort you as needed. He is your counselor and leads you into all truth. He is your strength and waiting on the inside of your heart for you to call upon Him as needed in your life.

Every addict struggles with temptation at some point, just like every Christian struggles with sin, for addiction is just another attribute of sin. The flesh is a personal problem for everyone and will continue to be a personal problem from cradle to the grave. Nevertheless, we all want to avoid the sorrow and pain sin causes, and now we can because we have Jesus and the power of the Holy Spirit living on the inside of us, so now that which so easily drew us into sin and bondage, no longer has the power to control us.

Ephesians 5:17-18 **"Therefore do not be foolish, but understand what the Lord's will is. Do not get drunk on wine, which leads to debauchery. Instead, be filled with the Spirit."**

Now that we are empowered by the Holy Spirit, we gain victory through our knowledge of Christ. Our faith, hope and trust in a God greater than ourselves allow us the power to prevail over our circumstances. The Holy Spirit is the great comforter, the most powerful person in your life and it is your job to trust God with all your heart, and lean not own your own understanding. Do not always seek to understand it. Simply have faith and hope, trust God and understanding will come.

A Winning Attitude

It is time to focus all of our circumstances away from ourselves and concentrate on Jesus. It is time to realize how immensely blessed you are. God has overlook all your flaws and forgiven you of all your sins. Today, you are blessed beyond measure with the gift of His grace. The same spirit that lived on the inside of Jesus now lives in you.

Hebrews 12:2 **"Fix our eyes on Jesus, the author and perfecter of our faith."**

Only by looking onward, do we begin to appreciate why our past was necessary for our edification. The confusion is now gone and with great clarity you can begin to comprehend why you are here and where you are headed. From this point forward, your attitude will determine your destiny.

My once negative attitude made my life feel like a raging storm with all sense of hope fading in the dismal sea, the waves and torrents were beyond my control. I felt trapped, afraid, and alone. I tried outrunning it, but there was no escape. To escape the storm would mean, I would have to escape from myself, for I was the storm, and the true nature of its existence lived on the inside of me. As I began drowning in the anguish of stormy waters and all I could see in my unforeseeable future was death, in desperation, I cried out to go God.

Jesus not only calms the physical seas, but He can also calm the seas within our soul and mind, and when you come out of the storm, you will not be the same person you were when you walked in. You will be filled with God's spirit and His spirit compels us to seek more about Him through His word, which will have a persuasive impact on our thoughts and actions.

Glory to God my prayers were heard. I reached out to God with a sincere heart. I called out from the depths of my soul, for I had absolutely nothing to lose. I opened my heart, and I invited Jesus in. With that invitation, came the divine power of the Holy Spirit. I turned to the Bible, adamant on being up close and personal with the man known as Jesus Christ.

<u>Philippians 4:13</u> "All things are possible through Christ who strengthens me."

Besides, my life was depending on it. And sure enough, it was through the word of God that I was completely transformed. I was able to find the essential strength necessary to overcome addiction.

<u>Proverbs 23:7</u> "For as he thinketh in his heart, so is he..."

Maintaining a positive attitude regardless of your circumstances is the key. How you perceive things and how you interpret situations is largely dependent upon how you view life. If you are viewing life with negative thoughts and a defeated attitude, you open the door to fear, anxiety, disappointment, frustration, and insecurities. However, if you choose to maintain a positive attitude, it allows room for growth and your spiritual eyes are opened. You will start to look beyond what you see and begin trusting what God has promised you in His word. A winning attitude is the characteristics of someone walking in victory with a prudent spirit. Therefore, with Christ Jesus at the helm, we win daily.

John 15:7 "If you remain in me and my words remain in you, ask whatever you wish, and it will be done for you."

As I continued to embellish on the scriptures, my thought process began to transform, my outlook on life changed, and I was able to adjust the way I perceived life. I learn that if I take God at His word, that word will stand in times of trials. It took courage and it took faith, but I'm' doing it. I was bold enough to apply God's word to my life and that is when my entire life completely changed.

Deuteronomy 31:6 "Be strong and courageous. Do not fear or be in dread of them, for it is the LORD your God who goes with you. He will not leave you or forsake you."

The Bible is God's word to us and provides a broad perspective on how to deal with life, not on our terms, but on God's terms. Being that I am a new creation in Christ, my outlook on life changed dramatically. Where I was once in a never ending cycle of desperation, despair, and utter hopelessness, has now changed to an endless cycle of recognizing that I indeed stand victoriously. Each minute of every hour, and every hour of each day I remain clean and sober, I win. Today, I win daily because I lay my petition before the Lord. Victory is found when we turn our eyes to God and allow Him to operate on our behalf. In battle, you may lose control of a situation, but if those battles bring us to a point of total surrender unto God, we will always win spiritually.

Positive Affirmations

Repetition is the key to making positive affirmations effective in your life. These affirmations would be a list of positive qualities about yourself, but more importantly, the promises of the scriptures from God's word. I recommend repeating them when you wake up every morning, meditating on them throughout the day, and repeating them once more before going to bed at night. Make a visible list of your positive affirmations, writing them down in a journal, taping them to the refrigerator or the bathroom mirror. Do whatever you must to keep them in visible view until they are planted firmly in the core of your heart as you become able to meditate on them throughout the day from memory.

The more you repeat them the more you begin to accept them about yourself and your life. Pretty soon those thoughts become actions and you begin to live your life based on the divine characteristic of Christ.

You are no longer tempted by the world because God's word has become an active being in your daily living. You are able to arrest every thought that is not like Christ and take it captive, transforming negative thoughts into positive affirmations based upon the promises of God's word.

2Corinthians 10:5 "We demolish arguments and every pretension that sets itself up against the knowledge of God, and we take captive every thought to make it obedient to Christ."

I just want to point out that it is all well and good to quote scriptures, but if you do not actively apply them to your daily life, they become of no value. Even as a Christian, not every thought is going to be in line with God's will and purpose, but now that the Holy Spirit lives within us, we are able to take captive negative thoughts and bring them into the obedience of Christ. As we focus more and more on God's word, we begin to realign our thinking with that of God's, casting negative thoughts that hinder us over to Him

1 Peter 5:7 "Cast all your anxiety on Him because He cares for you."

Allow God to rid you of fruitless distractions so that you are able to put more focus on living God's truth and enjoying the gift of recovery.

Matthew 13:22 "The one who received the seed that fell among the thorns is the man who hears the Word, but the worries of this life and the deceitfulness of wealth choke it, making it unfruitful."

So if you find yourself stuck in negative thinking or any thoughts distracting you from your goal to attain salvation, sobriety, and a new way to live, take those distractions and cast them over to God.

The key to casting distractions and negative thinking over to God is replacing them with positive affirmations written in God's words. As you do so, there is a God given sense of peace that surpasses all understanding and set itself guard over your heart and mind.

Philippians 4:7 **"And the peace of God, which transcends all understanding, will guard your hearts and your minds in Christ Jesus."**

God's peace is what guards our heart from worry, fear, and anxiety. And because we have decided to surrender our lives over to His care, we are blessed with the unwavering confidence knowing that God is faithful to do all He has promised in His word.

Hebrew4:16 **"Let us draw near with confidence to the throne that we may receive mercy and find grace to help us in times of need."**

For this very reason, we pray for God's knowledge and understanding that we may not be lead astray by the devices of Satan. When doubt starts to seep in your mind, or you feel that God is not presently helping your situation. You must take action not allowing yourself to be controlled by feeling, but rather by faith. Don't be controlled by what your circumstances look like, but rather by faith. Don't be controlled by what other people tell you, but rather by faith. For we walk by faith and not by sight.

2 Corinthians 5:7 **"We walk by faith, not by sight."**

For this reason, we get up and take a stand because our faith is rooted in God's word. Below, I have listed several positive affirmations to get you started.

Isaiah 40:29 **" God gives me power when I am worn out and strength when I am weak."**

Matthew 19:26 **"With God in my life, all things are possible."**

John 15:2 **"Jesus keeps pruning me so that I will be even more productive for God."**

Psalm 139:14 **"I am fearfully and wonderfully made by God."**

James 4:8 **"As I draw near to God, He draws near to me."**

Hebrews 12:10 **"God's discipline is always good for me because it means I share in His holiness."**

Proverbs 4:20-22 **"I keep God's words in my heart. They are health to my whole body."**

John 6:63 "It is God's Spirit that gives me eternal life. My human effort accomplishes nothing..."

Romans 8:31 "God is for me so no one can ever be against me."

2 Chronicles 16:9 "God strengthens me because my heart is fully committed to him."

Isaiah 41:10 "I do not fear because God strengthens me."

1Peter 5:5 "I defeat this evil world by trusting Christ to give me victory."

Philippians 4:7 "Through prayer, the peace of God guards my heart & mind."

\

The Journey of Endurance

There have been many of times in my life when I just wanted to give up and quit. My life had become completely unmanageable. I was totally overwhelmed with the consequences of my addiction, and the excruciation of my pain was unbearable. Every time I would make a stand to get back on my feet, my addiction would rise up against me with vengeance. The depth of my bottom was getting deeper and deeper. I felt as though it was impossible to dig my way out. But glory to God, today I stand as a living testimony there is indeed hope for those who are still sick and suffering. It is not a crime to get knocked down in life, but it is a failure not to get back up and demonstrate what you have learned from your experience and how that experience has changed you for the better.

Throughout your life you can expect to face various storms, and for the most part, they are not going to be very enjoyable, but above all else, do not quit. When faced with incredible hardship, never give up, never stop believing, and never stop learning from your experiences. I want you to understand that each storm is designed to shape you into the person God desires you to be. It is through those tough and trying times that you are being refined, tested, and strengthened. God is building your character as He allows the endurance of your faith to be tested. It is time to dig deep within your spirit and know that you are more than a conquer.

<u>Romans 8:37</u> "No, in all these things we are more than conquerors through him who loved us."

You were created to rise above your circumstances. The storm will not last forever, those urges will go way, and the test of temptation will pass. Just hold on knowing the reward of salvation is yours when it is all said and done. Your trust has a great recompense and your only hope of salvation is by enduring, but you must remain faithful, never lose hope, and always trust that God will see you through the adversities of life. Success is not something that is going to come easy, but I assure you that you can win and live triumphantly over addiction.

I'm praying for you to finish the course of this life victoriously. If you quit, you lose it all. You lose your family, your self-respect, and your life, but more importantly, you lose your hope of salvation. Don't you ever quit, don't you ever give up! If you are currently burdened with discouragement or confusion, put your faith in God and His eternal word. He will help you overcome and give you victory in every aspect of life.

"**Battles are fought in our minds every day. When we begin to feel the battle is just too difficult and want to give up, we must choose to resist negative thoughts and be determined to rise above our problems. We must decide that we're not going to quit. When we're bombarded with doubts and fears, we must take a stand and say: "I'll never give up! God's on my side. He loves**

me, and He's helping me! I'm going to make it*!"*
<u>**Joyce Meyer**</u>

You are certain to preserver because the power of God resides on the inside of you. When we commit ourselves to God and the truth sustained through God's word, we find that life is now tolerable, and a life with Jesus Christ is a worthy reward.

<u>**Hebrews 12:1-2**</u> **"...And let us run with endurance the race God has set before us. We do this by keeping our eyes on Jesus, the champion who initiates and perfects our faith."**

It is to be considered joy when we meet trials of various kinds. God has emphasized repeatedly throughout the Bible that we do not have to be overtaken by temptation or trials. He has equipped us with the strength to endure the suffering we experience.

Unfortunately, there are many who begin the commencement of the race, but fail to run with endurance. They succumb to their fleshly desires as they quickly become exhausted with the process and are therefore consumed by the agony of addiction. Satan's mission is to see that me, you, and the rest of the world fails, never finishing the race of endurance and that you are inadequately prepared to fight the good fight. He has led many to believe salvation is unattainable and has enticed them with the pleasures of sin. However, we must remain focused, keeping our eyes on the prize, looking to God the author and finisher of our faith, and He will strengthen us to endure to the very end.

Therefore, it is time you begin magnifying the promises of God's word and not the problem.

Galatians 5:24 **"Those who belong to Christ Jesus have crucified the flesh along with its passions and desires."**

Secular counseling such as N.A. and A.A. are great programs, and they do a good job of treating the symptoms of our addiction. However, addiction is indeed a spiritual problem, an internal conflict that can only be resolved though the knowledge of God's word. The Bible teaches us that we will become powerful by learning and applying Biblical truths and principles. The person of the Holy Spirit utilizes the word of God to renew are thinking. Therefore, allowing us to be permanently set free from the strongholds of addiction. However, if we are to indeed be renewed, we must hate what we once loved, for substance abuse is life dominating and self destructing, which cunningly creates an alternative reality composed of lies and deceit, craftily manipulating us into believing drugs and alcohol is a sensible solution to everyday problems while patiently masterminding our demise. It is unrealistic to believe you can have the best of both worlds. We must relinquish one and embrace the other.

Though giving up the use of life hindering substances is an enormous achievement, abstinence alone is not an end to a means. In order to ensure a permanently successful recovery, we have to be committed to the changes that can only be found through the study of God's word. It is important that you study and learn by the revelation of God's word, and utilize the power of the Holy Spirit to avoid temptation and sinful influences. Otherwise, you will continually find yourself stuck in a place of defeat and perpetual failure, with no strength to resist sinful urges.

This is the benefit and power of God's word as a real heart change occurs and motives, thoughts, and attitudes are transformed, altering our behaviors in a positive way that not only benefits the recovering addict, but also society as a whole.

"The greatest discovery of my generation is that a human being can change his life by changing his attitude."
<u>**William James**</u>

You must read, memorize, study, and meditate upon the Bible, allowing yourself to be fully controlled by the Holy Spirit. We have power in the names of Jesus to renounce the strongholds of addiction. Therefore, clothe yourself with the spiritual armor God gives His people through the power of the Holy Spirit:

Ephesians 6:10-11 "Finally, be strong in the Lord and in his mighty power. Put on the full armor of God, so that you can take your stand against the devil's schemes."

- **The belt of truth** – You shall know the truth and the truth shall set you free. Jesus is the way, the truth and the life.
- **Breastplate of righteousness** – Is our assurance that the birth, death, and resurrection of Jesus enable us to stand righteous before the Father.
- **Feet of readiness** – Always be prepared to share your story. The freedom you received in Christ must be shared with others.
- **Shield of faith** – We are enhanced with the necessary strength to shield off temptation and unwarranted urges put into operation by Satan.
- **Helmet of salvation** – You must guard your mind against enemy intrusion.
- **Sword of the spirit** – Faithfully studying God's word and skillfully putting Biblical truths into action.
- **Praying in the spirit** – When you pray in accordance with God's spirit, you can pray according to God's will and be confident of His perfect answer to your request.

If you are to have any success over addition and the many adversities presented in this life, it is going to take replacing unhealthy thoughts and behaviors with new and healthy ones. That means completely letting go of any and all life hindering substance, activities, and people, and begin honoring the self-sustaining knowledge of God's word. Self-control is a fruit of the spirit and a skill that can be developed and improved upon over time as you become more acquainted with the knowledge of God. However, if you continue living a life of irresponsibility, if you continue playing the victim, then you deny the great truth that life in of itself is a choice. A choice to live clean and sober, a choice to live morally correct, a choice to finally take a stand and not be defeated by addiction.

A person of faith does not wake up the same person they were yesterday, for they have learned to use their faith as oil to take the friction out of life, stumbling blocks are used as stepping stones, and liabilities become assets. They have learned to master the moment of unexpected detours as they have become persons of irrefutable character. Though character is not something we are born with, it is something that can be developed as we experience trials and adversity, for you are not impervious to the troubles of the world because you are now a child of God who is clean and sober. Bad things are going to happen, but it is how you choose to respond to those bad things that are going to define your character. Adversity is the very tool needed to develop the fruit of our character by providing circumstances in which we are tempted to express the exact opposite.

"Seeds of faith are always within us; sometimes it takes a crisis to nourish and encourage their growth."
<u>**Myles Munro**</u>

Let us begin this transformation process by acknowledging your past mistakes as learning experiences that have now become a part of the monumental change taking place inside of you this very moment. Something amazing is happening as this book comes to a close. You are starting to believe in yourself as you begin living the truth with a new and discerning perspective controlled by divine insight, losing what you cannot keep while gaining what you cannot lose.

"Stop watering things that were never meant to grow in your life. Water what works, what's good, what's right. Stop playing around with those dead bones and stuff you can't fix, it's over...leave it alone! You're coming into a season of greatness. If you water what's alive and divine, you will see harvest like you've never seen before. Stop wasting water on dead issues, dead relationships, dead people, a dead past. No matter how much you water concrete, you can't grow a garden.
<u>**TD Jakes**</u>

As you continue meditating on the word of God, you will be transformed by the renewing of your mind. When that happens, the chains that once bound you to addiction are broken, and you are then set free, but sometimes creating such new images of hope is tough, especially when there are old images of doubt and discouragement blocking the way. Though it may take a while for you to see yourself prospering in God, let me encourage you to fight the good fight as you endure the journey. You can do it, if you remain steadfast in the word.

<u>2Peter 1:3</u> **"His divine power has given us everything we need for a godly life through our "knowledge of him" who called us by his own glory and goodness."**

Beware, whenever the chains of addiction are been broken or a stronghold of any nature has been demolished, that same spirit misses being your master and will attempt to seduce you into letting it back in. Even though it no longer has control or influence over you, it will still harass you with tempting thoughts. Satan will begin planting seeds of doubt as you begin wondering if any real hope of recovery exists.

However, as a believer, you are gifted with the divine power of Jesus Christ. You can remain free of these influences by taking captive harassing thoughts and making them obedient to Christ. You do not have to listen to Satan's lies. Your life has been empowered by God's grace and the power of His spirit to accomplish what would normally be humanly impossible.

The key to victory over addiction is found in the knowledge of God. Submission to God is not a recovery program, it is a lifestyle.

Made in the USA
Middletown, DE
30 August 2021

46800998R00047